SMUGSHOT

Pop Culture in Caricature

SCOTT PERRY

All illustrations by Scott Perry

All rights reserved. No portion of this book may be reproduced in any form without permission from the publisher, except as permitted by U.S. copyright law.

ISBN: 9-798218-455774

© 2024, Scott Perry

AN INTRODUCTION

I've been drawing caricatures since I was a little kid. Spurred on by MAD magazine's Mort Drucker and Jack Davis, my first "likenesses" were of Charlton Heston and Barbra Streisand.

From there, I went on to lampoon my teachers and friends, eventually ending up sketching in the gift shop of a Ramada Inn one afternoon.

Years later, after my years in the advertising and publishing world, I heard of a project in which artists around the world were taking part. The challenge was to create one piece of art every day for 100 days — drawings, watercolors, photography, digital imagery — and post them on social media. The challenge was not only to entertain followers, but to see how much creative stamina an artist could wield. Being a pop culture junkie, naturally caricatures are where my mouse and keyboard landed.

Here are my 100 images from 100 days. Enjoy.

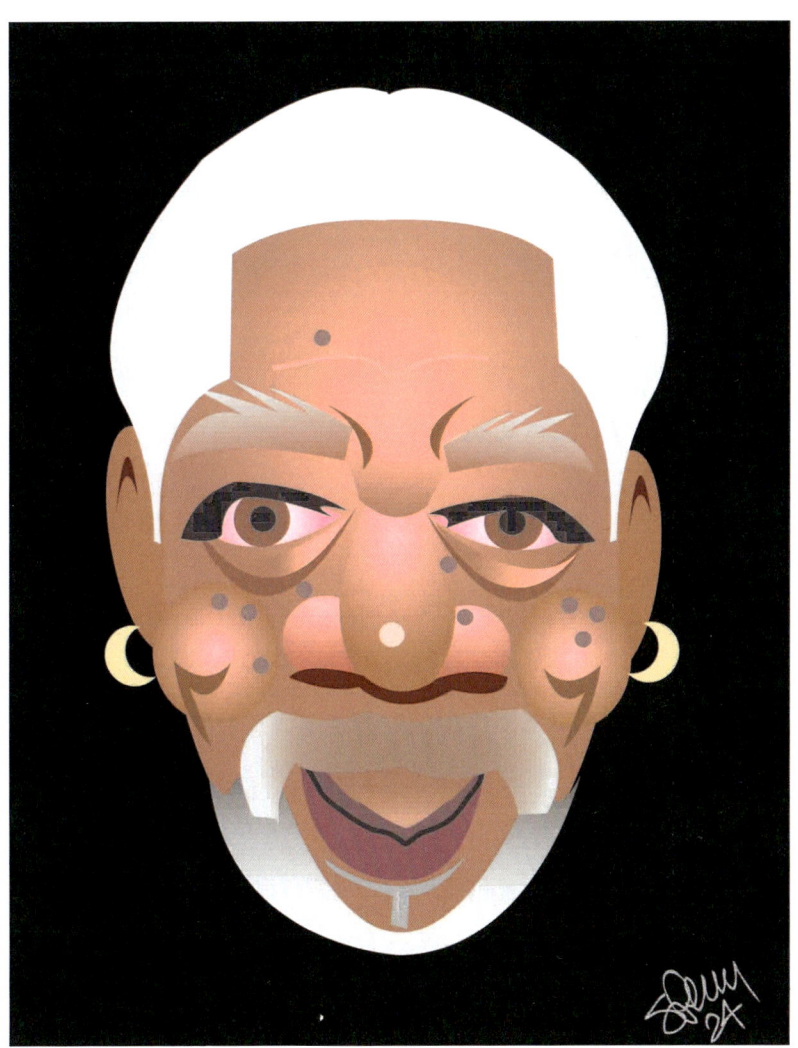

WHO'S WHO?

1	Willie Nelson	25	Marty Feldman
2	Leonardo DiCaprio	26	Divine
3	Liza Minnelli	27	Gloria Swanson
4	Don Knotts	28	Barbra Streisand
5	Stevie Wonder	29	Timothée Chalamet
6	Robin Williams	30	Daniel Radcliffe
7	Snoop Dogg	31	The Golden Girls
8	Freddie Mercury	32	Mama Cass
9	Cher	33	Jim Henson
10	Maggie Smith	34	Reba McEntire
11	Bob Ross	35	Janet Leigh
12	Lady Gaga	36	Mr. T
13	Joan Crawford	37	Dolly Parton
14	Bette Davis	38	Jamie Farr
15	Sylvester Stallone	39	Ian McKellen
16	Taylor Swift	40	Paul Lynde
17	Marlin Perkins	41	Lawrence Welk
18	Bernadette Peters	42	Elijah Wood
19	The Beatles	43	Catherine O'Hara
20	Morgan Freeman	44	Graham Chapman
21	Patti Lupone	45	Ann B. Davis
22	Anderson Cooper	46	Jacqueline Kennedy
23	Jan Brady	47	Mr. Whipple
24	Elton John	48	Tim Curry

#	Name	#	Name
49	Gilligan's Island	75	Whoopi Goldberg
50	Luciano Pavarotti	76	Billie Eilish
51	Bob Marley	77	Lady Elaine Fairchilde
52	John Denver	78	Liberace
53	Granny Clampett	79	Lily Tomlin
54	Roddy McDowall	80	Peter Dinklage
55	Julia Child	81	Tammy Faye Bakker
56	Charles Nelson Reilly	82	Angela Lansbury
57	Jenna Ortega	83	Orville Redenbacher
58	Carol Burnett	84	Lucille Ball
59	Formerly Known as Prince	85	Elvis Presley
60	Formerly Known as Prince	86	Michael Jackson
61	Awkwafina	87	Pee Wee Herman
62	Beyoncé	88	Cloris Leachman
63	Audrey Hepburn	89	Gilda Radner
64	Peter Sellers	90	Gene Wilder
65	Ruth Buzzi	91	Malcolm McDowell
66	Donny & Marie Osmond	92	Jackie Chan
67	Rowan Atkinson	93	Agnes Moorhead
68	Fred Rogers	94	Fantasy Island
69	Tina Turner	95	Lin-Manuel Miranda
70	Mick Jagger	96	Jeff Goldblum
71	Mike Tyson	97	RuPaul
72	John Belushi	98	Karen Black
73	Johnny Depp	99	Spider-Men
74	Judy Garland	100	David Bowie